BUILD YOUR BUSINESS

# START YOUR CRAFTING BUSINESS

*by Mary Meinking*

CAPSTONE PRESS
a capstone imprint

**Snap Books are published by Capstone Press**
**1710 Roe Crest Drive, North Mankato, Minnesota 56003**
**www.mycapstone.com**

**Library of Congress Cataloging-in-Publication Data**
Name: Meinking, Mary, author.
Title: Start your crafting business / by Mary Meinking.
Description: North Mankato, Minnesota : Capstone Press, [2017] | Series: Snap
   books. Build your business. | Includes bibliographical references and index.
Identifiers: LCCN 2016048258| ISBN 9781515766902 (library binding) | ISBN
   9781515767022 (ebook (pdf))
Subjects: LCSH: Handicraft—Marketing—Juvenile literature. |
   Selling--Handicraft—Juvenile literature. | Small
   business—Management—Juvenile literature.
Classification: LCC HF5439.H27 M45 2017 | DDC 745.5068/1—dc23
LC record available at https://lccn.loc.gov/2016048258

## EDITORIAL CREDITS

Editor: Gena Chester
Designer: Veronica Scott
Media Researcher: Kelly Garvin
Production Specialist: Laura Manthe

## PHOTO CREDITS

Shutterstock: Africa Studio, 13, Antonio Guillem, 29, bikeriderlondon, 24, Catalin Petolea, 20, Cressida studio, 9 (inset), Diana Hlevnjak, 17, DragonPhotos, 1 (bottom left), Ekaterina Pokrovsky, 23, faber1893, 28, Iakov Filimonov, 15, 22, Lera Efremov, 18, Mariia Khamidulina, 1 (right), Marinerock, 3, Monkey Business Images, 5, MPFphotography, 25, NataSnow, 21, OnlyZoia, 6, 14, Paul Matthew Photography, 12, photocell, 2, Rawpixel.com, 16, 26, Rock and Wasp, 11, Sedgraphic, 10, Siryk Denys, 18, Syda Productions, 27, Vladimir Melnik, 7, Vladimir salman, 8–9, Zadorozhnyi Viktor, cover

Artistic elements: Shutterstock: Art'nLera, grop, Chief Crow Daria, jolly_photo, Marie Nimrichterova

Printed and bound in China.
004725

# Table of Contents

INTRODUCTION

# INTRODUCTION
# BEYOND CRAFT TIME

From jewelry to decorations, the options for crafts are endless. Do you have a talent for crafting? Have you ever thought about selling your unique craft items? It might be easier than you think! Many people prefer unique handmade items over factory-made goods. And you could be the one selling them those goods.

You will have many roles in your crafting business. You'll not only be a crafter, but also an advertiser, a salesperson, and a customer service specialist. Many of these skills will help you later in life. The creativity and hard work you put into your crafts can make your business dreams come true!

## Tip

Many people learn crafting skills through family members, friends, or by taking classes. Learn other crafts by reading books or watching online videos. But nothing perfects your skills like practice.

CHAPTER 1

# CREATE THE NEXT CRAFT CRAZE

## What Craft to Make?

You may already have a great idea for your craft business. If not, what kinds of crafts do you like making? Or better yet, what things interest you? If you like being on your phone, maybe you'd like to make cell phone cases. If you have good penmanship, maybe you could showcase your talent by making decorative signs.

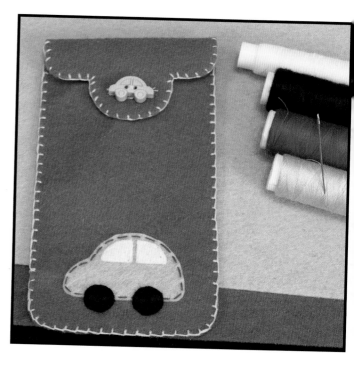

Will your craft item be wearable, useful, or just nice to look at? Wearable creations can be anything from jewelry to clothing. Useful crafts are things such as handbags, shelves, or scarves. But some customers are drawn to crafts just because they are beautiful or unique. They'll buy creations that can hang on their walls or be displayed in their yards.

Maybe it's time to try a new craft technique or use different materials. Are there extra things around your house that could be used to create something wonderful? Maybe there are old game pieces, food containers, or CDs that can be re-purposed. Look in the recycling bin or in nature for possible craft materials.

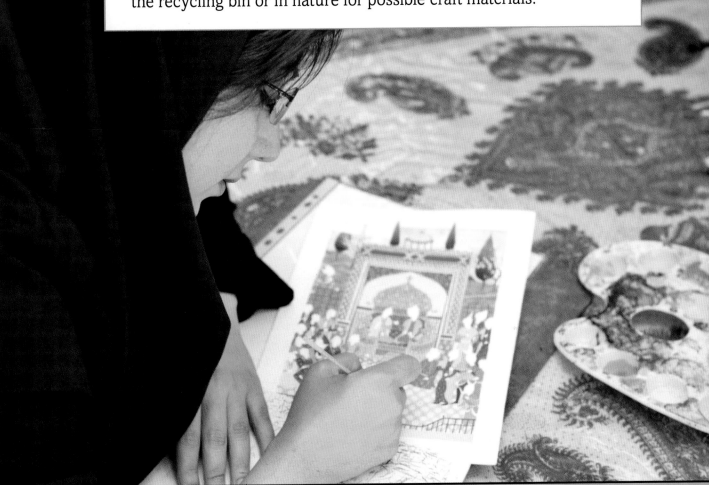

**Tip**

Still stumped? Think about the things you and your friends like to buy. Could you create them instead?

## Borrowed Inspiration

If you're still stuck on what craft to make, look at the handiwork of others. Use their creations as a starting point for your own work. Look online, in books, or at craft fairs to see what's popular. Etsy, an online craft store, is a great place to start your search. But remember not to copy anyone else's products. Many crafters use the basic idea of others and play around with it. They rework it until it becomes different enough to be considered their own design. You too will need to come up with your unique twist.

Most importantly, create a craft item you enjoy making! Be sure you can make hundreds of them without getting bored.

Choosing a craft **medium** is equally important. And you have many options, including wood, beads, fabric, metal, or paper.

Tip

Pet owners love their pets! If you love them too, you could make personalized pet dishes, leashes, collars, or clothes. Pet crafts are in high demand. In 2016, U.S. pet owners spent more than $60 billion on their pets!

**medium**—the materials or methods used by an artist

# Ask Around

Once you've chosen which craft item to make, create several samples. Choose your best four or five items and perfect them. Maybe they are different color combinations, designs, or styles.

Poll your friends and family in what big companies call a "focus group." Gather them together or ask them individually which one of your designs they like best. Would they buy it or think it would sell? What would they change to make it better?

**Tip**

Talk to others in businesses similar to yours. See what they charge and where they sell. Maybe they'll share their tips and secrets to business success with you.

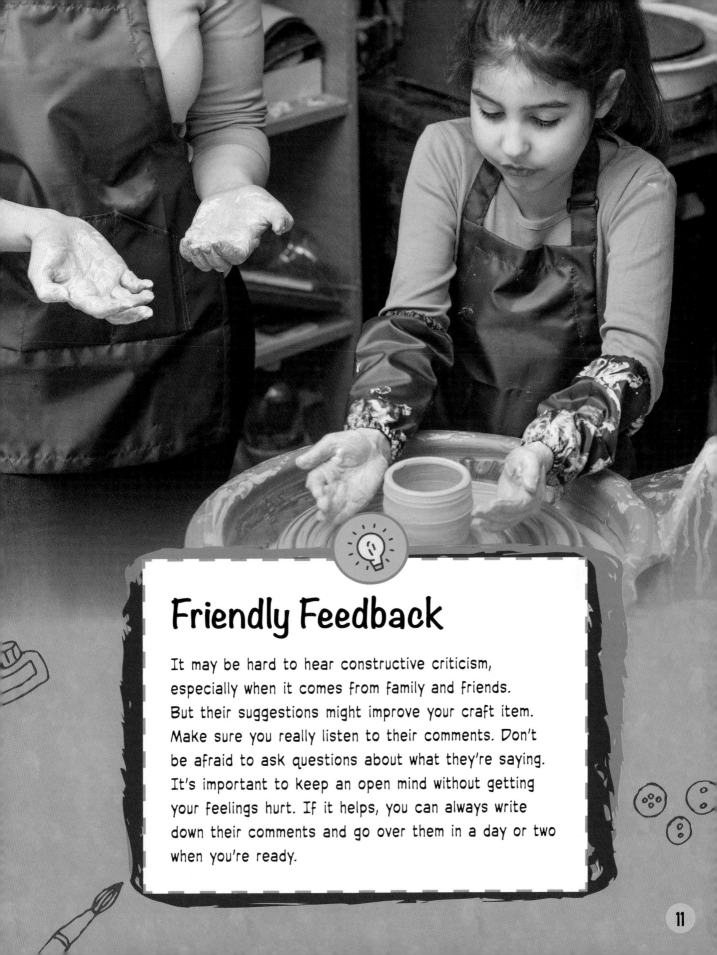

# Friendly Feedback

It may be hard to hear constructive criticism, especially when it comes from family and friends. But their suggestions might improve your craft item. Make sure you really listen to their comments. Don't be afraid to ask questions about what they're saying. It's important to keep an open mind without getting your feelings hurt. If it helps, you can always write down their comments and go over them in a day or two when you're ready.

CHAPTER 2

# PRODUCTION LINE

## The Birth of a Workshop

You will need to find a spot to create. Working in your bedroom or on the kitchen table might seem like a good option. But it really depends on what you plan to do. If your craft involves painting or sanding, your work area could get messy. It would be better to work in the garage or in another area where messes would be easier to clean up.

The ideal workshop is an undisturbed, well-lit work area. Add a folding table or an unused desk to your workspace. This will give you a place to dry or assemble many parts.

You will also need storage for your supplies and tools. You could use plastic bins or shoeboxes. Keep it organized. Your materials should be separated from your finished products.

Make sure your workshop is functional. But more than that, make sure it's a place you enjoy. You'll be spending a lot of time on your craft, and working in a drab space isn't good motivation. Decorate it with your favorite pictures or quotes — anything to jump-start your creativity and imagination.

**Tip**

Make sure your workroom has good ventilation. Open a window if you work with paints or materials that have strong fumes.

## Start Small and Stick with It

When you first start out, start small. Only buy enough supplies to make a few of each item. Then see what sells. That way you won't end up with a lot of leftover materials you'll never use.

If your items don't sell, don't give up! Starting small also allows you to start over. You can change your craft to make it more appealing to customers. Do you need to adjust the color, size, or design? Remember no one's first attempts are masterpieces.

One of your short-term goals should be to cut costs and work faster to make as much money as possible. But your most important goal should be to have fun. Making money doesn't mean much if you don't enjoy what you do.

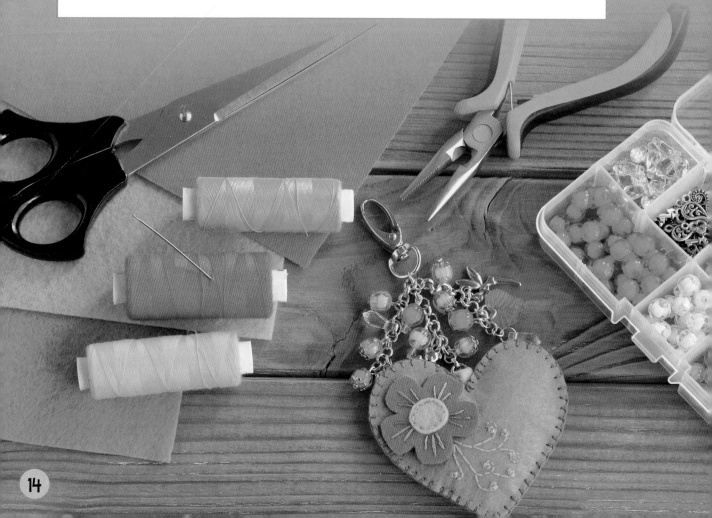

# Buying Supplies

Once your product is selling steadily, buy larger quantities of your supplies in **bulk**. Buying in bulk means paying more upfront. But in the long run, the overall cost of materials to make each product can be cut by as much as 30 to 80 percent!

Most bulk distributors are available online. If you want to order from an online company, you'll need to ask your parents for help. Most websites require a credit card for payment.

## Tip

In your business you are bound to make mistakes. Your success depends on how you recover from these mistakes so that you can avoid them in the future.

**bulk**—a large amount

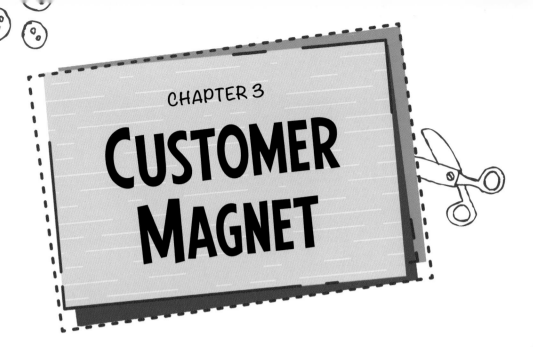

# CHAPTER 3

# CUSTOMER MAGNET

## What's in a Name?

One of the most important business decisions you make will be the name of your business. It's the first thing customers learn about you. Here are some tips to consider:

- Pick a short, catchy name. But don't reveal too many details. You might not want your customers to be able to guess exactly what you make. Be a little mysterious with your name, and customers will likely be interested in finding out more.

- Use your name in combination with your product. If you sell handmade rings, something like "Jessica's Jazzy Jewelry" might be a great option.

- Combine words to explain what you make. For example, if you make shampoo for dogs you could call your business "Shampoodles."

# Design a Logo

Once you've come up with a name, you'll want an eye-catching **logo**. A logo serves as a representation of your business. Your logo should include your business name with an image or icon. Use it in your **advertising**, packaging, and signs.

Choose a **typeface** that goes along with your craft style. Would a flowing script or a blocky typeface fit better? Be sure any images used in the logo relate directly to your business or craft.

You could draw your own logo. Or if you have access to a computer, you could design it digitally. Or ask a friend or family member to design it. You could possibly trade their logo design for some of your crafts.

**Tip**

Choose a color scheme for your advertising. Stick to only using those few colors. Use them on your printed materials, website, and booth displays.

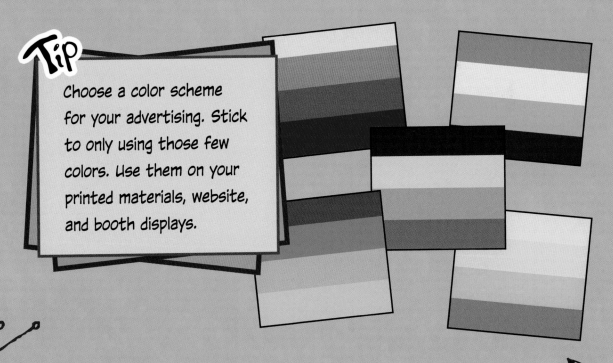

logo—a visual symbol for a company

advertise—to give information about something you want to sell

typeface—a set of letters and numbers that are all used in the same style and that are used in printing

# Promote Your Business

Like commercials on television, you need to **promote** your business. Let people know about your product. Your business can only make money if your customers can find you!

One of the best ways to advertise is to make flyers or brochures that show off your craft items. Flyers are flat sheets of paper printed on one side. Brochures are usually printed on both sides, and then folded. Think of them as mini catalogs. These will help your customers understand what you make.

You can also create business cards. These cards should have only your business name or logo and your contact information, such as your phone number or your email address. Always remember to get your parents' permission before giving out any personal information.

Wonderful Watercolors
Amy Smith 555-3971

**Tip**

An easy way to promote your craft business is by wearing or using your products.

# Brochure Basics

An ideal brochure is easy to read, and its design should reflect your craft style. In it include your business name, logo, and contact information. For safety purposes do not include your home address. Instead list the places your product can be found, such as craft stores, websites, or fairs.

Brochures almost always follow the same format, and free templates can be found online. Many brochures are folded into halves or thirds. On the inside panels, include clear color photos along with short descriptions of each product. If you have returning customers, you could include their short **testimonials** about your product.

It's best not to print prices in your brochure. That way if your prices change, you don't need to reprint your brochures too.

**Wonderful Watercolors**

**Amy Smith**
555-3971

**promote**—to make people aware of something

**testimonial**—a statement by a customer given in appreciation or gratitude toward a business

# CHAPTER 4

# SELL, SELL, SELL!

You've perfected your craft. You've advertised your business. Now all that's left is to sell your product!

## The Price Is Right

Customers are often willing to pay more for unique handmade craft products compared to generic store products. But how much should you charge? One good way is to see what your competitors are charging for a similar item and match that.

You could also use your **cost of production**. Determine how long it takes you to make one item, and multiply it by a fair hourly rate. Add to that the cost of all the supplies needed to make that item. Then add in 15 to 25 percent for your **profit**. This total is what you could charge.

# Who Are Your Customers?

To properly sell your product you need to know who will buy it. Are your customers men, women, or children? Are they tourists or locals? What are their ages? Each of these answers will help you decide how to advertise your craft.

### Tip

If your craft allows you to offer free samples, do so. This will help convince potential customers to buy your product.

**cost of production**—the amount of money it takes to make a product

**profit**—the amount of money left after all the costs of running a business have been subtracted

# Finding Local Customers

Setting up a craft booth is a great way to meet your customers face-to-face. You could have a booth or table at a craft fair, farmer's market, flea market, or county fair. But remember most places have regulations to follow and they charge a booth rental fee.

Another option is to sell at local stores on **consignment**. To do that, you'll need to set up an appointment with the store owners. Show them your craft products and give them the prices of your items. When your items sell, the store will usually keep about 20 to 60 percent of the price. If your items don't sell, you get them back.

You could also sell your items **wholesale** to local stores. When doing this, stores will buy your items from you upfront. They'll keep all the profits, and you won't get back the unsold items. To do this you'll need to contact the stores to show them your handiwork and give them your prices.

**Tip**

Sell at craft shows during fall and winter holiday seasons. Those are the best selling times of the year. Most crafters make half their annual sales during this time.

**consignment**—the batch of goods that is sent to a dealer, who only pays for what is sold and returns the rest

**wholesale**—the sale of goods in large quantity in order to resell for profit

23

# Finding Customers Online

You can reach new customers anywhere in the world through the Internet. Ask your parents if you can join an online craft mall site, such as Etsy. This is an easy, inexpensive way to sell crafts online. But these sites do take a percentage of your sales. Your parents will need to manage your account for you.

After you make a sale on the Internet, the payments commonly go through an online payment system, such as PayPal. If that is the case, you'll need to use your parents' bank account to get your money.

Internet sales can pile up quickly and unexpectedly. Check for online orders at least once a day. To make it easy to remember, block off a specific time each day to do this and make it your routine. You won't ever meet your customers face-to-face, so good communication is key. Always reply to customers as soon as you see their orders.

You should also make sure customer orders are delivered promptly. Crafts should be shipped out within two days. If it's a local order, try to deliver the craft within a day or two.

 **Tip**

Stay safe on the Internet. Don't go online or talk to customers without your parents' permission or supervision. And never give out your age or home address.

# Craft Your Website

If you have computer skills, you and a parent could build your own website to sell your crafts. Templates are also available to help build your site. You'll need to buy a **domain name** and pay an annual fee. Making your own site is a good way to eliminate a craft website from taking part of your profits.

Not only is a website a great way to sell crafts, it's also great advertising. Place your website address on flyers, brochures, and business cards. Make an "About" section to explain the story behind your business and help potential customers feel connected to its success. Your parents and other trusted adults might be willing to help you promote your website.

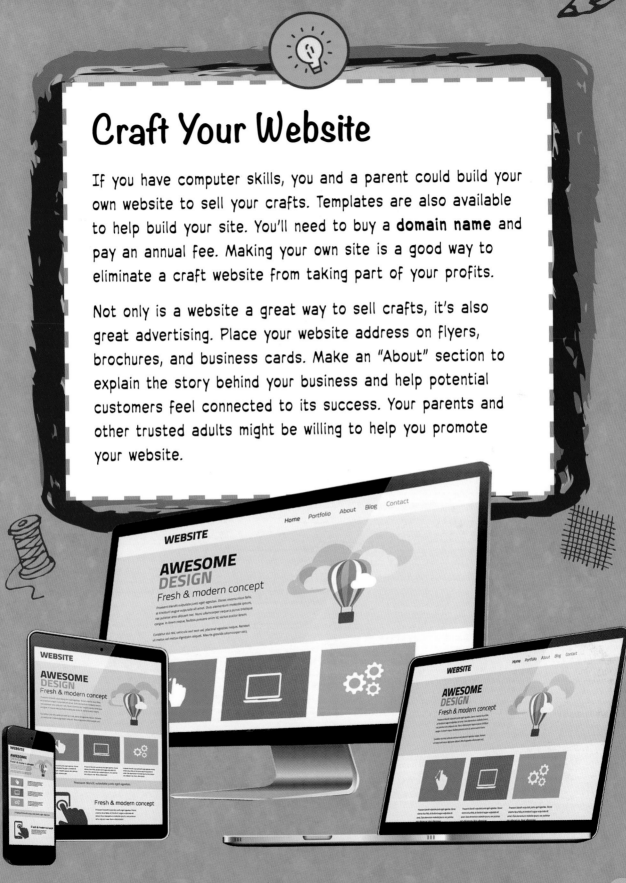

**domain name**—the characters that form the main part of an Internet address

CHAPTER 5

# BITS OF BUSINESS

## Happy Customers

Creating a successful crafting business doesn't happen overnight. It takes lots of time and hard work. Not only do you need to make a great product, you need to keep your customers happy. Satisfied customers will recommend your crafts to friends. Unsatisfied customers will also let others know you let them down.

You should act professionally and treat all customers with respect. Be polite to even the most difficult customers. Remember that they are paying you, so take their requests and problems seriously.

## Mistakes Happen

When problems arise, try to come up with a solution that keeps everyone happy. Maybe a product order is late, gets lost, or doesn't look like what was expected. Do your best to correct the problem.

You may need to discount the price, redo the order, or even give it to them for free. Sometimes apologizing can make all the difference. This small gesture can help them become repeat customers.

# Order Overload

As your business becomes a success, orders might come in one after the other. You may feel stressed if you promise more than you can deliver. Be realistic with how long it takes to make each of your products. Then multiply it by how many items are ordered. If you're not going to meet deadlines, you'll need to ask for help.

Enlist your friends and family. Train them on how you want tasks done. That way you can get your orders out quicker and not miss any deadlines. Never cut corners and send out a poorly made product.

# The Sky's the Limit

Spend your profits wisely. Are you saving up for college or to buy something special? Or are you putting money back into the business by buying more supplies or equipment?

It helps if you create short-term and long-term goals for your business. Where do you see yourself by the end of the year? By the end of five years? Write it down. Keep those goals in mind as your business progresses and you have more money to spend. Then enjoy accomplishing your dream of creating a successful crafting business.

**Tip**

A busy, successful business might start taking up more of your free time. Don't let it get in the way of school, time with friends, and other activities. A healthy balance is necessary to enjoy your crafting success.

# GLOSSARY

**advertise** (AD-vuhr-tize)—to give information about something you want to sell

**bulk** (BUHLK)—a large amount

**consignment** (kuhn-SINE-muhnt)—the batch of goods that is sent to a dealer, who only pays for what is sold and returns the rest

**cost of production** (KAWST OF pruh-DUHK-shuhn)—the amount of money it takes to make a product

**domain name** (doh-MAYN NAYM)—the characters that form the main part of an Internet address

**logo** (LOH-goh)—a visual symbol for a company

**medium** (MEE-dee-uhm)—the materials or methods used by an artist

**profit** (PROF-it)—the amount of money left after all the costs of running a business have been subtracted

**promote** (pruh-MOTE)—to make people aware of something

**testimonial** (TESS-tuh-moh-nee-uhl)—a statement by a customer given in appreciation or gratitude toward a business

**typeface** (TYP-fays)—a set of letters and numbers that are all used in the same style and that are used in printing

**wholesale** (HOLE-sale)—the sale of goods in large quantity in order to resell for a profit

# READ MORE

**Danielle, Tasha.** *Amina's Bracelets: A Kidpreneur Story.* Detroit, Mich.: Financial Garden LLC, 2016.

**Fields, Stella.** *Accessory Projects for a Lazy Crafternoon.* Lazy Crafternoon. North Mankato, Minn.: Capstone Publishing, 2016.

**McGillian, Jamie Kyle.** *The Kids' Money Book: Earning, Saving, Spending, Investing, Donating.* New York: Sterling Children's Books, 2016.

# INTERNET SITES

FactHound offers a safe, fun way to find Internet sites related to this book. All of the sites on FactHound have been researched by our staff.

Here's all you do:
Visit *www.facthound.com*

Type in this code: 9781515766902

Super-cool stuff! Check out projects, games and lots more at
**www.capstonekids.com**

# INDEX